This Book is a

GIFT

from

----

to

----

on the occasion of

----

date

When Your FOUNDATION *Needs* HEALING

Dr. D. K. Olukoya

WHEN YOUR FOUNDATION NEEDS HEALING
© 2013 by DR. D. K. OLUKOYA

ISBN - 978-978-920-066-5

A Publication of
Mountain of Fire and Miracles Ministries
Press House
13, Olasimbo Street, Off Olumo Road,
P.O.Box 2990, Sabo, Yaba, Lagos, Nigeria.
☎ 070-143-129-88, 070-165-589-81
Email: mountainoffireandmiraclespress@yahoo.com
Website: www.mfmbooks.co.za

Cover Illustration:
Pastor (Mrs) Shade Olukoya

1st Printing - January, 2014

*All Scripture quotations
are from the King James Version of the Bible.*

PREFACE

Many African men today have an ugly past. not necessarily because of what he himself did, though this may be part of it, but majorly as a result of what his forbears had done in the past.

Interestingly, the God we serve is the Alpha and Omega. He is not only the God of the present and the future, but of the past too.

The bible says in Lamentation 5:7, "our fathers have sinned and are not; and we have borne their iniquities"

Our past is our foundation, and the past is like a journalist, reporting us to the future. Our foundation can either make or mar our destines. Many people today have the right credentials and connections, but are not successful because of foundational problems.

The Bible says: "if the foundation be destroyed, what can the righteous do.."{Psalm 11:3}. The foundation of many have been destroyed on the altar of idolatry, fetishism, polygamy ,witchcraft, ritual sacrifices, deity and nature worship, murder, incest, slave trade et cetera. These kinds of foundation need the cleansing and the healing touch of the Almighty.

How you can solve the problems of faulty foundation, by using the right weapon of spiritual warfare to destroy satanic cobwebs is the theme of this book. I pray that as you read it, the Mighty Healer shall meet you at the point of your needs in Jesus' name.

Dr. D.K. Olukoya

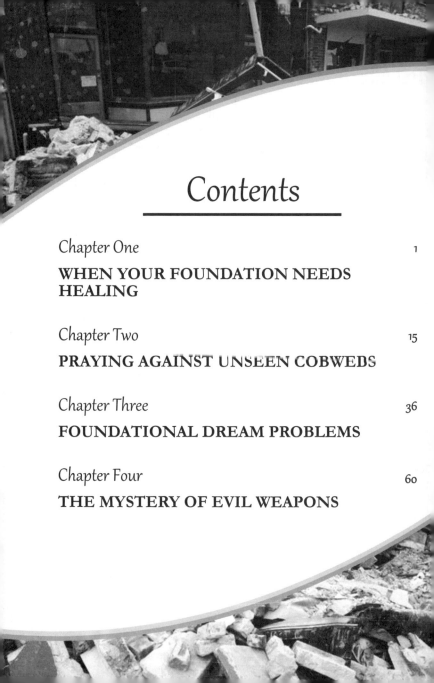

Contents

Chapter One

When Your Foundation Needs Healing

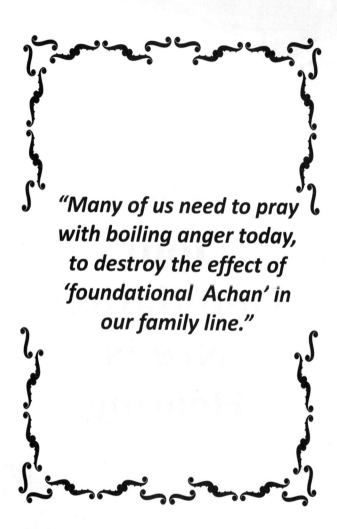

"Many of us need to pray with boiling anger today, to destroy the effect of 'foundational Achan' in our family line."

Joshua 7:1-8:

"*But the children of Israel committed a trespass in the accursed thing: for Achan, the son of Carmi, the son of Zabdi, the son of Zerah, of the tribe of Judah, took of the accursed thing: and the anger of the LORD was kindled against the children of Israel. And Joshua sent men from Jericho to Ai, which is beside Bethaven, on the east side of Bethel, and spake unto them, saying, Go up and view the country. And the men went up and viewed Ai. And they returned to Joshua, and said unto him, Let not all the people go up; but let about two or three thousand men go up and smite Ai; and make not all the people to labour thither; for they are but few. So there went up thither of the people about three thousand men: and they fled before the men of Ai.*

And the men of Ai smote of them about thirty and six men: for they chased them from before the gate even unto Shebarim, and smote them in the going down: wherefore the hearts of the people melted, and became as water. And Joshua rent his clothes, and fell to the earth upon his face before the ark of the LORD until the eventide, he and the elders of Israel, and put dust upon their heads. And Joshua said, Alas, O Lord GOD, wherefore hast thou at all brought this people over Jordan, to deliver us into the hand of the Amorites, to destroy us? would to God we had been content, and dwelt on the other side Jordan! O Lord, what shall I say, when Israel turneth their backs before their enemies!

verse 16 - 18:
So Joshua rose up early in the morning, and brought Israel by their tribes; and the tribe of Judah was taken: And he brought the family of Judah; and he took the family of the Zarhites: and he brought the family of the Zarhites man by man; and Zabdi was taken. And he brought his household man by man; and Achan, the son of Carmi, the son of Zabdi, the son of Zerah, of the tribe of Judah, was taken.

verse 24 - 26:
And Joshua, and all Israel with him, took Achan the son of Zerah, and the silver, and the garment, and the wedge of gold, and his sons, and his daughters, and his oxen, and his asses, and his sheep, and his tent, and all that he had: and they brought them

unto the valley of Achor. And Joshua said, Why hast thou troubled us? the LORD shall trouble thee this day. And all Israel stoned him with stones, and burned them with fire, after they had stoned them with stones. And they raised over him a great heap of stones unto this day. So the LORD turned from the fierceness of his anger. Wherefore the name of that place was called, The valley of Achor, unto this day."

F rom the passage above, we can see that a single man had committed an offense that affected the whole nation. A single man had done something wrong and it affected the whole of his lineage. Many of us need to pray with boiling anger today to destroy the effect of 'Foundational Achan'; the Achan in our family line.

Jericho was the first city to be conquered in the conquest of Canaan, they overcame that one miraculously. The second city to be attacked after Jericho was Ai. The spies who went to look at Ai recommended two or three thousand men, but these 3,000 men were beaten because there was sin in the camp and the guilty soul needed to be identified. It is amazing to note that the guilt of one man became a stumbling block to the progress of Israel.

The deed of one man blocked the progress of a whole nation. God puts an embargo on the city of Jericho before it was ever captured. He said no spoils were to be taken for the use of the Israelites. He said everything in that city were cursed and were to be destroyed, except the silver and gold vessels which were supposed to be the treasury of the Lord. Every other thing apart from those vessels were to be burnt. Achan went and took that which God said they should not take and this caused trouble down the line.

Foundations are very important in the spiritual realm. Every building or structure has a foundation. The foundation could be weak or strong, perfect or faulty. A building stands or falls based on the type of foundation it has. The story above is instructive. It reveals the power of a single foundational Achan.

The spirit of Achan is indeed a terrible spirit and a mother of many other terrible sins. Achan's sin did not only have magnetic capacity, it also had generational consequences. Although our past is gone and forgotten by many, but the past is not a sleeping dog that should be allowed to be. Our past is like a journalist reporting us to the future. We need to really deal with it.

I pray that every foundational Achan troubling your family shall be buried by the power of God today, in the name of Jesus.

DEEP FACTS

There are deep and mysterious facts in this matter:

1.   All trespasses are not detected instantly.

2.   Trespasses that a man commits in life are sometimes detected even after the person's death.

3.   Our sins can trouble other people, even to the level of generation yet unknown

4.   Sin will not only trouble a sinner, but it will have effect on a sinner's family. When Achan sinned, it did not only affect him, it also affected his family. The sin of one person can pollute all. Achan was from the tribe of Judah. Judah and

Benjamin were the principal warriors in Israel. Achan was a brilliant soldier, he did not die in the war, he escaped but he hid the garment where he thought God could not see it. Achan, the thief, did not die in the battle from where he stole. He believed that all was over and that nobody could detect him. Achan was so different from the man Jonah, who repented quickly. Achan took God for granted. The endurance of God is mysterious.

<u>DEAL WITH YOUR FAMILY ACHAN!</u>

The presence of an Achan in your family line may be why there is incurable diseases, constant losses, gradual dispossessions, constant health problems that swallow money, etc. That may be the reason why there will always be somebody in jail in that family. That may be why they are always stealing in that family and why they cannot stop stealing. That may be reason why some are carrying certificates about, but the certificates are unproductive. That may be why there is a mark of hatred on some people. That may be why there is backwardness and possessed children. There is an Achan that had done something wrong and it is causing trouble. That may be why there is academic disruption. That may be why there is this, "from grace to grass" syndrome.

There is something known as "the curse of the dispossessed". When there is an Achan in a family line, it is like leprosy that hangs upon everyone coming from that family. All curses issued by the dispossessed are acidic and potent. All curses of the dispossessed are generational. I feel really sorry for thieves and armed robbers because curses pursue them unto their death and will continue after their death. Beloved, there is a great problem in your hand if there is an Achan in your family line.

Now in Nigeria, most cars are 'tokunbo cars' (secondhand). So if you buy a tokunbo car, you need to anoint it and pray on it very well because you may actually be driving a stolen car. The curse of the dispossessed may be upon it.

HOW TO DEAL WITH THE ACHAN
IN YOUR FAMILY LINE

1. You need to surrender your life to Jesus.

2. You need to repent from all known sins.

3. You need to repent on behalf of your family line.

4. You need to attack the Achan spirit.

5. You need to repossess what this spirit has stolen from you.

6. You need to barricade your life so that this spirit

does not trouble your destiny anymore.

PRAYER POINTS

1. Lord, let Your healing power flow into every area of my body, relevant to conception and child bearing.

2. God who quickeneth the dead, quicken everything concerning my conception and child bearing, in the name of Jesus.

3. I bind, plunder and render to naught, every spiritual activity contrary to the peace of my home, in the name of Jesus.

4. Lord, let this month be my month in the name of Jesus.

5. Lord, let this month be our month in the name of Jesus.

6. Let my womb be purged by the fire of the Holy Spirit, in the name of Jesus.

7. Let all evil hands be removed from the affairs of my life, in the name of Jesus.

8. I cover myself with the blood of Jesus.

9. I break every covenant with any sexual demon, in Jesus' name.

10. I rebuke the spirit of the dog and cast it out of my ways, in the name of Jesus.

11. I place a wall of fire around my life, in Jesus' mighty name.

Chapter Two

─────────────

Praying Against Unseen Cobwebs

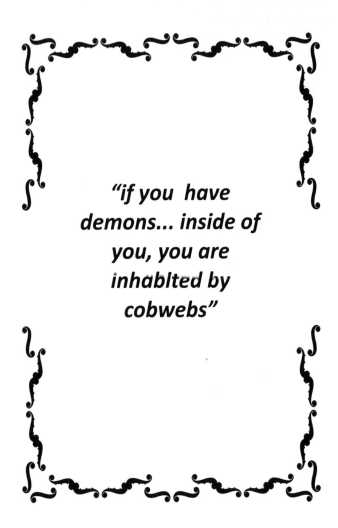

"if you have demons... inside of you, you are inhablted by cobwebs"

I n this chapter, we shall consider those sins that constitute cobwebs in people's lives:

1. **Those who want God to share them with something else:** When something else is sharing you with God, you are an adulterer.(Rev.2:22) Sometimes, the spirit of the Lord will come upon you and you will say, "Thus saith the Lord, do this and do that", then the same person who prophesied will still be getting angry. Prophecy and anger do not go together. This fact must be registered in your spirit today. You are an adulterer when you put up a holy attitude but inside, you are bad. It is a big insult for you to share God with something else. Are you completely holy and given unto Him? Hypocrisy means you sharing God with something else.

2. **Knowledge:** A lot of people believe that when they acquire university degrees, they are the most intelligent people and nobody else knows better. My advice to such people is to go and frame their certificates, hang them around their necks and go about with them. The irony of the situation is that, someone with a degree in one subject is a novice in another discipline or subject.

3. **Having sex outside marriage:** Having sex outside wedlock is adultery. You can have a woman or a man at home and still be an adulterer or adulteress. This happens when you just put a woman in your house without marrying her, without paying her dowry and living in an unholy wedlock.

<u>WAY OUT</u>

1. **Take time to be holy:** Anything in your life that is not holy makes you to an adulterer.

2. **Read, digest and meditate on the word of God:** Every Christian must have a plan for Bible reading everyday. The excuses that you always have a busy day at work and that you are tired at night and in the morning are not acceptable to God. If you fall down and die one day in that working place that you are always running to, somebody else will be employed to replace you and that company will not collapse because of your demise.

Beloved readers, think about it; why are you starving the inner man and feeding the body that will not go beyond this planet, thereby punishing the eternal for the temporal? You must have a regular Bible-reading timetable. If you are so confused and do not even know where to read, go and buy 'Our Daily Bread' or 'Daily Guide' or 'Daily Manna.' There are so many good devotional books in all Nigerian languages.

3. **You have to be a prayer addict:** If something else is contesting with your prayer life, that means that you are an adulterer. The Bible says: "Pray without ceasing." (I Thess. 5:17) If you are not praying at all, you are not just disobeying God, you are also an adulterer.

Anyone who breaks any of the ten rules of Christian living listed below is playing with hidden spiritual sin cobweb.

1. **Complete obedience to God:** Total obedience. This means you are ready to d, whatever God tells you to do no matter what it takes.

2. **Trust the Lord with all your heart and lean not on your own understanding:** always commit all your ways to God. let your own will dissolve in His own will

3. **Do not be a hypocrite:** The story of that woman caught in the act of adultery tells us a lot about the nature of man. Although the Bible does not write what Jesus wrote on the ground, the Bible says: "Speak evil of no man." (Titus 3:2) If you want to smear someone else with mud, you will first of all stain your own hand. It is a powerful force that hinders us and it is the force of hypocrisy. Hypocrites are counterfeit Christians. A counterfeit is a corruption of the original though he looks like the original, talks like the original and dresses like the original. Although hypocrites were so close to Jesus

physically yet they were far away from Him
Spiritually.

4.   **Speak evil of no man:** If you are going to see
     good days, keep your lips from speaking guile
     and do not talk evil of anybody. The bad things
     you are using your mouth to say about others is
     another key to spiritual adultery.

5.   **Stop judging or criticising others:** Know that
     you are not perfect, but only trying to be. Take
     a look at yourself, that song writer says: "Take a
     good look at yourself and you will see others
     differently." So, it is time for you to check
     yourself. The sins that we have in our nature
     make us needful of God's abundant mercy.
     The Bible says: ***"If thou shall mark iniquity, O
     Lord, who can stand?"*** (Ps. 130:3) No one could
     rightfully throw stone at that woman.

Something darkens the heart of men and their knowledge, they want to criticise others and say all kinds of things; they want things exposed in others, while they want their own sins to be hidden. This is why beloved, evil society should have no place in any church, it creates problems.

God did not create us in the same way and we do not do things in the same way. It is therefore, a terrible thing to be saying bad things about other people. It is a sign of spiritual adultery and it will not help you in the way God wants you to live.

6. **Consider your body as the temple of the Holy Spirit:** Immediately you begin to do anything against your body, you annoy the Holy Spirit

and this make you an adulterer. You can sin against the Holy Spirit and you can also grieve and quench the Holy Spirit, when you do not consider your body as His temple. Your body is not for fornication nor adultery, it is the temple of God. The Bible says that whoever will pollute the temple of God, him will God destroy. (Ezek. 36:18)

7. **Have a firm control over your thought life:** You have to be very careful over your thought pattern. Make sure you do not think evil. Those who have vagabond thinking pattern think anything. When you do not have a firm control over your thoughts, then you inadvertently give access to evil thoughts which will cripple your spiritual growth.

8. **Be a witness for Christ anywhere you are:** If you are hiding your Christianity because you do not want people to say that you are a fanatic, then you are an adulterer.

9. **Neglect not the assembly of each other:** If you neglect the house of God, you are an adulterer. When you spend your time attending to friends or entertaining people when you should be in the church, then you are an adulterer. Those are not the kinds of friends you should have anyway Your friends should be those who will be ready to follow you to church. You should not have friends that drink alcohol. When you serve people alcohol and they commit a sin or misbehave you are guilty of the same offence even if you claim that you did not partake in it with them

10. **Be filled with the Holy Ghost:** If you are not filled with the Holy Ghost, that space that is left unfilled will be occupied by something else because there is no vacuum in nature. If you fill your cup to the brim with water, you cannot put any other thing in the cup. So when you are filled with the Holy Ghost, there will be no space for any other spirit to enter.

The problem of spiritual cobwebs needs to be tackled because of its consequences. What are spiritual cobwebs? Let us identify them.

If you are breaking any of these ten rules, then you are an adulterer, but there is a way out beloved- run back to your "Husband". (II Corin. 11:2) If you have sold yourself to the enemy, God can buy you back from the enemy's market with the precious Blood of His Son. (Rev. 12:11)

1.   **Worship of modern-day idols:** All those who are worshipping modern-day idols are adulterers. An idol is anything you place before God or besides God. In this modern times, there are about five idols that men worship in hypocrisy.

a) **Pleasure:** People now claim to enjoy themselves outside Christ.   Many Christians now take pleasure in leaving the church premises for the beach to relax, enjoy and socialise with one another, particularly during Easter or Christmas seasons. It is a pity that this is happening. Why are they doing this? It is because they have not seen the revelation of Jesus. There are many things that people are now wasting time on e.g. television, internet, computer games, etc. These have polluted many lives and they are tools the enemy is using seriously. However, thank God there are many Christian programmes on television now.

b) **Money:** People now worship money as if it is the only thing that exists and matters. mammon is the god of money , and Christ Said you can not serve God and mammon (Mathhew 6:24)

c) **Another idol of the modern-day world is power:** People are ready to die for power in order to control and dominate their fellow men.

2. **Cobwebs of the heart:** Addiction to alcohol, smoking, bad habits, etc. are indications that you are a spiritual adulterer, if such things are still sharing you with God. There are many idols sitting in the temple of the human heart, many

have demons playing there. If you have demons playing inside of you, you are surrounded by cobwebs.

Jesus is not coming for an unclean Church; that is why the Bible calls demons unclean spirits. He will not take you with those unclean spirits, they must therefore go. If you say that your Maker is your husband, cry to the Lord in prayer at this moment.
Pray this way: *"O Lord, do not divorce me, in the name of Jesus."*

This prayer point is very important and you must treat it that way.

THE WAY OUT

1. **Repentance:** Repentance involves everyone, nobody is left out. You need to check the situation you are in right now and change for

the better. Make a decision and God will back you
up. Are you sharing God with something else,
you need to repent now!

2. **Discipline:** You must learn spiritual discipline,
that is, to keep you under the discipline of God.
Paul said: "I put my body under, I bring it under
subjection lest at the any time after I have
preached to others, I myself will be a cast
away."

3. **Deliverance:** You know that there are certain
things in your life that should go. Do not be shy
or afraid. Explain to those that can help you, no
matter how shameful the thing is.

Sometimes in the past, a woman came to me for
counselling. Her story was stunning and pathetic.
She opened her bag and brought out a candle. She
said whenever she was in a place for few minutes,

something would order her to go to the ladies. She would then use the candle to excite herself sexually. If she did not do this, she would "not be okay". She was a married woman with four children. If she had not revealed her problem, who would have known how to help her?

Are you just looking good, speaking good English, smiling at everybody and yet your "husband" is a candle? You need deliverance! The Lord sets her free and she burnt the candle. Many people are doing sinful things like that and they are covering them up with nice dresses, not telling anybody. How will you be free? Do you want to wait for the devil to use it against you? Is it not better for one or two people to know about the problem and help you and you find your way to heaven, than for you to hide it and delay your deliverance?

You must understand your authority in God. I have t

been invited to many places to preach and the worst one was a church in Lagos, Nigeria. They said they were holding a seminar on: "The second coming of Jesus", so I was happy. I was to be the speaker on the last day of the seminar. At that time, I had only one suit because prayer warriors do not wear suits. So, I went to dry-clean the suit, took my Bible and went to the church. With all the advertisement done on the seminar, the oldest person I saw sitting in the congregation was about 12 years old.

So I sat down there, looking overdressed. The few elderly people came in and introduced me. I did not know where to start. I came expecting to teach the second coming of Jesus to old and young people alike led by the Spirit of God. So, I read from the Book of Zephaniah 1:14 which says;

> *"The great day of the Lord is near, it is near and hasteth greatly, even the voice of the day of the Lord; the mighty man shall cry there bitterly"*

Immediately I read the first verse, all the rich people took their Bibles and they went out. Later, I discovered that this was not in the programme, they just wanted to use the forum to collect money from the people. This is sheer hypocrisy in the house of God! Before hypocrisy could be institutionalised, the individual members would first of all have become hypocrites. If human beings can brand you like that, I hate to see what God will write about you. I know that my Redeemer and my Maker is my husband and I do not want a divorce. On that day, I do not want Him to call you an adulterer because you shared Him with something else. The end of the matter is eternity. I want you to benefit here in this world and in the world to come.

<u>PRAYER POINTS</u>

1. Any area of my life that is friendly with God's enemy, I separate from you, in the name of Jesus.

2. O Lord, purge me clean with Your blood, in the name of Jesus.

3. I refuse to be trapped by satanic cobwebs, in the name of Jesus.

4. O Lord, I am a so, so, and so, ... I refuse to deceive myself. Help me Lord!

5. O Lord, help me to recover my wasted years, in the name of Jesus.

6. I remove my name from the register of failure, in Jesus' name.

7. Let every limitation to my life be come to an end, in Jesus name.

8.   I reject the spirit of lukewarmness, in the name of Jesus.

9.   I paralyse every power distracting me from the gospel of Christ in the name of Jesus.

10. I command every evil influence over my life to be neutralised, in Jesus' name.

11. Father Lord, give me the grace to focus on Jesus all the time in the name of Jesus

12. I destroy the activities of beggarly powers against my life, in Jesus' name.

Chapter Three

Foundational Dream Problems

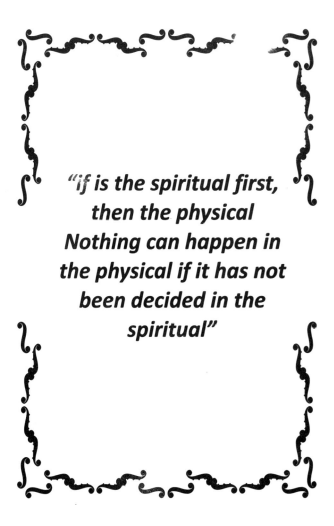

"*if* is the spiritual first,
then the physical
Nothing can happen in
the physical if it has not
been decided in the
spiritual"

S ome of the toughest foundational problems are problems that are rooted in satanic dreams. Unknown to many people today, dreams have been used to initiate multitudes into poverty.

Poverty is one of the most wicked weapons used by the enemy to harass millions of people all over the world. Poverty is a curse while prosperity is a blessing. Poverty is not just a state' it is a spirit. It is a satanic emissary on an evil assignment. When the spirit of poverty is at work, a lot of things would go wrong. The devil makes use of the spirit of poverty to subject multitudes to deplorable existence. Dreams are major tools through which he achieves this.

A girl was telling us about all what she did to her father's business. She said that whenever her father brought home a cheque, she would take the cheque, put it within her legs and then take it to their evil meeting and the father would not just know how he spent that money. We have had cases of people burying their fathers' monies in the ground. The fact that this is possible shows you that it is basically a spiritual thing.

This message should be taken seriously. The devil afflicts people with poverty dreams. These dreams come in different ways:

1.   Dreams in which a person spends money lavishly, like pasting money on the foreheads of women dancing on the streets or at parties.

2.   Dreams of finding yourself buying things in the market after receiving some money.

3.   When you dream of walking about barefooted, wearing rags or tattered shoes, or you see yourself as a beggar.

4.   If you are a trader and you see yourself in the dream having your wares unsold after putting them out for sale.

5.   If you dream that your properties are being auctioned in your presence.

6.   If you dream and see your pocket leaking or somebody stole some money from you or you lost some money and after looking for it, you never found it before you woke up.

7.   If you have ever dreamt that rats are running around your house, whether big or small ones: For instance, if you have about 700 logrammes

kilogrammes of 'gari' (cassava grain flour) in the house and there is only one rat around, the rat will seriously waste the gari. The rat will not finish the gari immediately; it will be taking it little by little and after some time, it will give birth to little ones that will be feeding from it as well. The gari will be reducing until it finishes.

8. If you dream of your purse being stolen or you find yourself with counterfeit money.

If any of these is happening in your life, then your dreams call for serious spiritual warfare. The devil goes around with the spirit of poverty because he wants people to serve him. He knows that when people are poor and they do not have sufficient money, they will go and serve evil spirits just to get money. I am yet to see anyone who has gone to receive money

from the devil who has not paid the ultimate price
for it. The devil does not have any free gift. He
operates a primitive trade-by-barter system.
The only free gift we have is in the Lord Jesus
Christ, given to us by God. Even if you try, you
cannot pay God back for His goodness.

We should get it clear that the devil has no free gift,
so we must recognise that anything that is existing
in the physical can be blocked or hindered in the
spiritual realm as well. Actually, it is the spiritual
first, then the physical. Nothing can happen in the
physical if it has not been decided in the spiritual.
So, it is possible that the totality of the money a
person will make in his entire lifetime can be
spiritually removed on the day that he or she was
born. The spirit of poverty will stay in such a life and
begin to operate therein. Even, if it does not
manifest immediately, it will certainly manifest
later.

I have seen many whose names were made popular by records that artistes waxed for them, who are now poor because the spirit of poverty took its toll on them.

The following signs show that the spirit of poverty is at work in a life:

1. When someone has sufficient income and is still having problems financially.

2. Inability to keep a regular job.

3. Inability to eat the normal food others are eating: Such people may have been told either medically or otherwise to stop eating some food items, thereby making them the cosumer of expensive foods.

4. Inability to control child-bearing and thereby sending the children to bad/substandard schools.

5. When you are always being duped or regularly attacked by thieves.

6. When you are surrounded all over by poverty-stricken relatives and you are their only benefactor.

7. Debt: Believers should cut down or totally avoid owing people money, especially the ones they know may be difficult for them to pay back.

8. The spirit of gambling is another sign of the spirit of poverty: The devil will be telling you; "Play again and you will win", but you end up losing. You may even keep doing it until you have lost all your possessions.

9.   When a man patronises prostitutes.

10. Health problems which require a lot of money.

11. When you keep registering for the same examination again and again without success.

12. If you lack promotion and your properties are frequently destroyed.

When all these things are happening, then you must learn the art of aggressive praying. However, instead of praying, a lot of people blame several other things and leave the actual agent alone.

When I was in the university, I used to feel sorry for some girls who spent all their money on clothes and make-up items without feeding well. Since their bodies were not sustained, they usually ended up breaking down.

When a man brings out a biro and a piece of paper to calculate what his wife bought from the market, there is no point in fighting him, he just needs deliverance from the spirit of poverty.

Ecclesiastes 6: 1- 2 reads thus:

"There is an evil which I have seen under the sun and it is common amongst men. A man to whom God had given riches wealth and honour so that he wanteth nothing for his soul of all that he desireth, yet God giveth him not power to eat thereof, but a stranger eateth it: this is vanity and it is an evil disease".

We know the story of Rockefeller. Rockefeller was a billionaire, but there was a time in his life when all he could eat was milk and crackers (biscuits). The money he had was useless to him. It was still the same spirit of poverty that tormented him.

In Isaiah 65:22, we read the stand of God on some issues:

"They shall not build and another inhabit. They shall not plant and another eat; for as the days of tree are the days of my people and mine elect shall long enjoy the work of their hands."

So, not enjoying the fruits of one's labour is caused by the spirit of poverty. God warned the children of Israel against disobedience. He told them that if they disobeyed Him, the spirit of poverty would be released upon them - Deuteronomy 28: 30-44:

"Thou shalt betroth a wife, and another man shall lie with her: thou shalt build an house, and thou shalt not dwell therein: thou shalt plant a vineyard, and shalt not gather the

grapes thereof. Thine ox shall be slain before thine eyes, and thou shalt not eat thereof: thine ass shall be violently taken away from before thy face, and shall not be restored to thee: thy sheep shall be given unto thine enemies, and thou shalt have none to rescue them. Thy sons and thy daughters shall be given unto another people, and thine eyes shall look, and fail with longing for them all the day long: and there shall be no might in thine hand. The fruit of thy land, and all thy labours, shall a nation which thou knowest not eat up; and thou shalt be only oppressed and crushed alway: So that thou shalt be mad for the sight of thine eyes which thou shalt see. The LORD shall smite thee in the knees, and in the legs, with a sore botch that cannot be healed, out of bitterness from the sole of thy foot unto the top of thy head. The

LORD shall bring thee, and thy king which thou shalt set over thee, unto a nation which neither thou nor thy fathers have known; and there shalt thou serve other gods, wood and stone. And thou shalt become an astonishment, a proverb, and a byword, among all nations whither the LORD shall lead thee. Thou shalt carry much seed out into the field, and shalt gather but little in; for the locust shall consume it. Thou shalt plant vineyards, and dress them, but shalt neither drink of the wine, nor gather the grapes; for the worms shall eat them. Thou shalt have olive trees throughout all thy coasts, but thou shalt not anoint thyself with the oil; for thine olive shall cast his fruit. Thou shalt beget sons and daughters, but thou shalt not enjoy them; for they shall go into captivity. All thy trees and fruit of thy

land shall the locust consume. The stranger that is within thee shall get up above thee very high; and thou shalt come down very low. He shall lend to thee, and thou shalt not lend to him: he shall be the head, and thou shalt be the tail."

THE CURSE

This is the operation of the spirit of poverty. These are the various manifestations of that spirit which can lead to sickness or death. As a believer, if you take no action, then nothing good will happen to you. Some families are under a definite curse and each person is affected. Even when they get to the point of making it, something will go wrong and everything falls apart again and no one is really getting anywhere. Until that curse of poverty is broken, the spirit of poverty will remain in place. Any member of that family struggling to make it will just fade away like a weak flame before a strong wind. However, believers who are in this situation can do something about it.

When ritual-money is used to start a business, the business will be in trouble. Some jobs are under a curse and until you break that curse, the spirit will still be in operation. Sometimes, when a person is wrongfully dismissed from a company, out of bitterness, he or she may place a curse on the company and this can put the company in trouble. If the owner of a company, e.g., the Chairman or the Managing Director keeps harassing his female staff sexually and they give in because they do not want to be sacked, the curse of poverty will immediately come upon the man and his company. The evil emptier-spirit will carry all his money back to the demonic world. All these things can be broken today, if you repent and do something about it, things will change for the better in your life.

THE THEFT OF POTENTIALS

The problem with many is buried potentials. One of the principles of success in life is to identify your God-given potentials and to use them. The spirit of poverty has blinded many people and is therefore stealing their potentials. Your God-given potential may be in your voice, memory, ability to organise things, business acumen, ability to understand and speak languages, analytical mind, ability to convince others, musical talents, powerful brain or foresight. Identification and development of these potentials are essential for a successful life.

Unfortunately, the potentials of many have been removed, giving room to the spirit of poverty to operate. Those buried potentials must be exhumed today, in Jesus' name. The spirit of poverty has used many parents against their children. A boy may begin to build houses with clay at a very tender age and the parents will keep warning the boy to stop doing so, thereby stopping the boy's architectural potentials from manifestation Many even warned their female children never to think of doing a job which they considered meant for men alone.

If a child starts drawing pictures, he or she is warned to stop it as it is considered an unserious vocation. The devil has deceived many parents into believing that there are only three honourable professions, which are: Medicine, Law and Engineering. This erroneous belief has planted the seed of the spirit of poverty in many families. The Bible as a very complete book shows us the gateways to poverty. The gateways are as follows:

1.   **STINGINESS:** Proverbs 11: 24-25 says: ***"There is that scattereth and yet increaseth and there is that withholdeth more than is meet,***

but it tendeth to poverty. The liberal soul shall be made fat; and he that watereth shall be watered also himself"

So, if you are stingy, you need to pray to be delivered because it is a gateway to poverty.

2. **LOVERS OF SLEEP AND SLUMBER:** Proverbs 20:13: *"Love not sleep, lest thou come to poverty; open thine eyes and thou shalt be satisfied with bread."*

If you need to set the alarm clock before you can wake up and pray, then you really need to do so.

3. **FOLLOWING VAIN PERSONS:** Proverbs 28:19: *"He that tilleth his land shall have plenty of bread: but he that followeth after vain persons shall have poverty enough."*

This act too leads to poverty.

The curse of The Law is in threefold - POVERTY, DISEASE AND DEATH. Christ came to redeem us from all these. So, today in your life is a day of powerful breakthroughs. If you have decisions to make or sins to repent from, start doing that now, so that you can break the evil stronghold in your life.

4. **LAZINESS:** Proverbs 10:4: *"He becometh poor that dealeth with a slack hand. But the hand of the diligent maketh rich."*

Laziness is a terrible gateway to poverty.

5. **MOCKING THE POOR:** Proverbs 17:5: *"Whosoever mocketh the poor reproacheth his maker and he that is glad at calamities shall not be unpunished."*

6. **FAILURE IN TITHES AND OFFERING:** Malachi 3:8-12 says that people who fail to pay their tithes and offerings rob God. This act is the surest way to poverty.

7. **NOT CONTRIBUTING TO GOD'S WORK:** Haggai 1:6-8 *Says Ye have sown much, and bring in little; ye eat, but ye have not enough; ye drink, but ye are not filled with drink; ye clothe you, but there is none warm; and he that earneth wages earneth wages to put it into a bag with holes. Thus saith the LORD of hosts; Consider your ways. Go up to the mountain, and bring wood, and build the house; and I will take pleasure in it, and I will be glorified, saith the LORD.*

8. **GIVING TO GOD IN SMALL MEASURES:** Luke 6:38: *"Give and it shall be given unto you, good measure, pressed down and shaken together and running over, shall men give*

> *unto your bosom. For with the same measure that ye mete, wither it shall be measured to you again."*

Remember this always that with the same measure that you give, it shall be given to you.

9. **ENGAGING IN THE WRONG BUSINESS:** You will find examples of this in the word of God. Luke 5:1-10 is a good example.

10. **NOT GIVING TO THE POOR:** You will find that in Proverbs 28 27.

REDEMPTION FROM THE CURSE OF POVERTY

" Christ has redeemed of us form the curse of the law, being made a curse for us: for it is written, cursed is everyone that hangeth on a tree..." Galatians 3:13

God has little interest in the economic situations of the country. What He is interested in is that in whatever environment He has placed you, you must be a blessed person. It does not matter if things are difficult in that environment, even if there are problems around, as a child of God, you must not be a partaker of the problems.

The Lord is ready to reach out to you today, but you must first draw His attention. Heaven is ready to open up to you if you bombard it with your prayers. Remember that God is not the author of evil. The person to fight is the devil and not God, your tenants, your colleagues or family members. With every aggression in your spirit, pray the following prayer points.

PRAYER POINTS

1. Lord, locate and revive all my buried potentials today, in the name of Jesus.

2. I break the curse of poverty in my life, in the mighty name of Jesus.

3. Spirit of poverty, I rebuke you and I bind you, in the name of Jesus.

4. Every spirit drinking the blood of my blessing, I bind you, in the name of Jesus.

5. every anti-blessing spirit in my destiny, I bind you now in the name of Jesus.

6. all satanic and witchcraft curse of poverty in my life, expire!, in the name of Jesus

7. Heavens of my prosperity, my wealth and abundance begin to open, in the Jesus name.

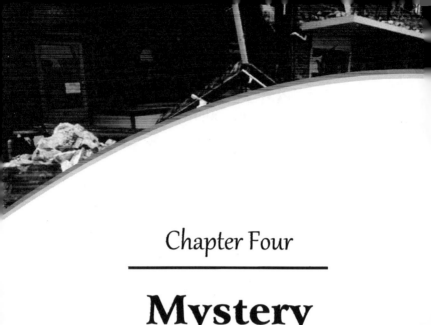

Chapter Four

Mystery
of
Evil
Weapons

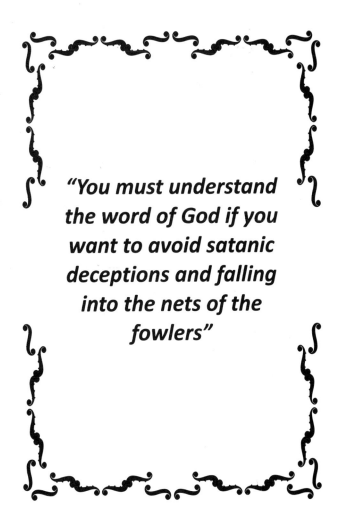

"You must understand the word of God if you want to avoid satanic deceptions and falling into the nets of the fowlers"

O ne of the weapons used by the enemy is the weapon of evil snares. Snares are used by the devil to capture unstable souls.

2 Peter 2:9-19:

"The Lord knoweth how to deliver the godly out of temptations, and to reserve the unjust unto the day of judgment to be punished: But chiefly them that walk after the flesh in the lust of uncleanness, and despise government. Presumptuous are they, selfwilled, they are not afraid to speak evil of dignities. Whereas angels, which are greater in power and might, bring not railing accusation against them before the Lord. But these, as natural brute beasts, made to be taken and destroyed, speak evil of the things that they understand not; and shall utterly perish in their own corruption; And

shall receive the reward of unrighteousness, as they that count it pleasure to riot in the day time. Spots they are and blemishes, sporting themselves with their own deceiving while they feast with you; Having eyes full of adultery, and that cannot cease from sin; beguiling unstable souls: an heart they have exercised with covetous practices; cursed children: Which have forsaken the right way, and are gone astray, following the way of Balaam the son of Bosor, who loved the wages of unrighteousness; But was rebuked for his iniquity: the dumb ass speaking with man's voice forbad the madness of the prophet. These are wells without water, clouds that are carried with a tempest; to whom the mist of darkness is reserved for ever. For when they speak great swelling words of vanity, they allure through *the lusts of the flesh, through much wantonness, those that were clean escaped from them who live in error. While they promise them liberty, they themselves are the servants of corruption: for of whom a man is overcome, of the same is he brought in bondage."*

Sin is a snare of the enemy. It might look interesting, nice, sweet and respectable, but when the snare starts to eat up its victims, it would devour without mercy.

Oftentimes, the devil would push someone to provoke a minister of God. If it is a minister that is not broken, he would just issue one or two curses on the person and that is all.

EVIL PRACTICES

Remember that Satan operated a successful music business and music is a very strong snare of the enemy. Check the type of the music you listen to. A believer who listens to worldly and perverted music will having serious spiritual problems. It is very saddening in Nigeria that the best-selling music is "Fuji music." Most of the wordings of this kind of music are absolute rubbish. All the music with bad inspirations are from the fowler.

All the women who borrow attires to put on for special occasions are walking into the traps of the fowlers. The devil has used this snare to introduce seeds of hatred into families. Reading books that promises power outside the Bible is another snare of the devil.

All the clever, satanic contributions targeted towards idol worship are snares of the fowlers. All the evil associations for market women and men are all snares. It is better to pray and quit such associations before the devil takes advantage of it to destroy your destiny. People who ignorantly proclaim, "Give unto Caesar what is Caesar's" make such statements to justify the evil snare of the devil that is entrenched in their lives.

Examine the foundation of the names you are bearing, they may be assisting the fowlers.

When somebody goes to satanic seers to find out what the future holds for him, the snares of the fowlers are already at work in such live Imagine the herbalist who starts to seek from cowries how your life would be? How can cowries, inanimate objects, start to "talk" about your future? What do you expect cowries to say about you? Do you not know that the demons have possessed the cowries to foretell the future? This will spell doom for such an inquirer. It is better to know the One who holds the future than to find out about the future.

When the powers of darkness set a trap and a victim falls inside, it is expected that the victim should come out of the snare fast. If not, they would kill the trapped.

You must understand the word of God if you want to avoid satanic deceptions and falling into the nets of the fowlers.

All forms of false doctrines that are rampant in the churches are snares of the fowlers. Baptism of babies is a snare of the fowler. Little babies cannot repent and confess their sins for they have not attained the age of accountability.

MARITAL SNARES

All forms of wrong doctrines on marriage are snares of the devil. For example, a man wants to marry and gets to his leader to make his intention known. The leader now asks, "Do you have girl-friends before?" The man says: "I had three of them before my conversion." The leader now asks, "Where is the first girl-friend?" And the man replies, "She is married and she is in America." The leader now says, "Unless you go and marry the former girl-friend who is now married to another person, then you have to remain unmarried!" What a false doctrine and what a snare of the devil.

FALSE HOPE

Any doctrine which convinces sinning Christians that they are going to heaven is a snare of the fowler. All these gimmicks and human manipulations to siphon money from the people of God are all devilish ploys and snares of the fowlers. Those who want to receive the Holy Spirit without being holy would only fall into the snares of the fowlers.

May God have mercy on people who believe that they are exonerated. Accumulation of knowledge above prayer life is a snare. They are ignorant of the fact that nowhere in the Bible are we commanded to exalt any aspect of Christian service above prayer. For the Bible says: *"Pray without ceasing."* (I Thess. 5:17) Prayer is the only thing to be done without ceasing. There is nothing like: 'singing without ceasing' or 'reading without ceasing' or 'preaching motivational messages without ceasing.'

It is amazing that some preachers are preaching saying that nobody could be holy for everybody is a sinner and it is only heaven that knows those who would be saved. I disagree. If you are saved you will know; if you are going to hell, something inside c your conscience will let you know. Although yo may try to deceive yourself, yet you will know th truth. Your conscience will always speak to yo secretly saying: "The position you are now qualifie you for hell fire."

FALSE DOCTRINES

Some people say, "there is no hell and there is n heaven" and that everything ends here on earth They say those whose conditions are better off ar in hell, those who are suffering on earth are alread in hell - these are doctrines of the devil.

Some are preaching on reincarnation, others allov all kinds of dresses to be worn to the house of Go as if God is celebrating a disco party. A womai comes into the house of God wearing what God say is an abomination a Jezebellian dress which expose the contours of the body and most of the men who are yet to be broken would be having inordinate feelings, for they would no longer concentrate on the word of God. this is a false doctrine that many churches are permitting today, but which is rather unfortunate.

Living in sin and expecting blessings to abound is a snare of the fowler. If you have been to the camp of the enemy to ask for help, it is a snare of the fowler.

We call such people 'those who warm themselves in the fire of the enemies' like Peter did. Surely, the bible says: *"He shall deliver thee from the snares of the fowlers..."* (Psalms 91:3)

PRAYER POINTS

1. I render null and void, such incantations and satanic prayers over me and my family, in the name of Jesus.

2. I retrieve this day out of the hands of the enemy, in the name of Jesus.

3. Spirit of favour, counsel, might and power come upon me, in the name of Jesus.

4. I shall excel this day and nothing shall defile me in the name of Jesus.

5. I shall possess the gates of my enemies, in the name of Jesus.

6. The Lord shall anoint me with the oil of gladness above others, in the name of Jesus.

7. The fire of the enemy shall not burn me, in the name of Jesus.

8. My ears shall hear good news, I shall not hear the voice of the enemy, in the name of Jesus.

9. My future is secured in Christ, in the name of Jesus.

10. My God has created me to do certain definite services. He has committed to my hands some assignments which He has not committed to anyone else. He has not created me for nothing. I shall do good. I shall do His work. I shall be an agent of peace. I will trust Him in whatever I do and wherever I am. I can never be thrown away or downgraded, in the name of Jesus.

11. Oh you element forces in the Heavenlies, you shall not hurt me by day or night, in Jesus' name.

OTHER BOOKS BY DR. D. K. OLUKOYA

1. 20 Marching Orders To Fulfil Your Destiny
2. 30 Things The Anointing Can Do For You
3. 30 Poverty Destroying Keys
4. 30 Prophetic Arrows From Heaven
5. 40 Marriages That Must Not Hold
6. 101 Weapons For Spiritual Warfare
7. A-Z of Complete Deliverance
8. Abraham's Children in Bondage
9. Basic Prayer Patterns
10. Be Prepared
11. Bewitchment musl Die
12. Biblical Principles of Dream Interpretation
13. Biblical Principles of Long Life
14. Born Great, But Tied Down
15. Breaking Bad Habits
16. Breakthrough Prayers For Business Professionals
17. Bringing Down The Power of God
18. Brokenness
19. Can God Trust You?
20. Can God?

OTHER BOOKS BY DR. D. K. OLUKOYA

OTHER BOOKS BY DR. D. K. OLUKOYA

40. Deliverance From Spirit Husband And Spirit Wife
41. Deliverance From The Limiting Powers
42. Deliverance From Evil Foundation
43. Deliverance of The Brain
44. Deliverance Of The Conscience
45. Deliverance By Fire
46. Destiny Clinic
47. Destroying Satanic Masks
48. Disgracing Soul Hunters
49. Divine Yellow Card
50. Divine Prescription For Your Total Immunity
51. Divine Military Training
52. Dominion Prosperity
53. Drawers Of Power From The Heavenlies
54. Evil Appetite
55. Evil Umbrella
56. Facing Both Ways
57. Failure In The School Of Prayer
58. Fire For Life's Journey
59. Fire for Spiritual Battles for The 21st Century Army

HER BOOKS BY DR. D. K. OLUKOYA

OTHER BOOKS BY DR. D. K. OLUKOYA

80. Looking Unto Jesus
81. Lord, Behold Their Threatening
82. Madness of The Heart
83. Making Your Way Through The Traffic Jam of Life
84. Meat For Champions
85. Medicine For Winners
86. My Burden For The Church
87. Open Heavens Through Holy Disturbance
88. Overpowering Witchcraft
89. Passing Through The Valley of The Shadow of Death
90. Paralysing The Riders And The Horse
91. Personal Spiritual Check-Up
92. Possessing The Tongue of Fire
93. Power To Recover Your Birthright
94. Power Against Captivity
95. Power Against Coffin Spirits
96. Power Against Unclean Spirits
97. Power Against The Mystery of Wickedness

HER BOOKS BY DR. D. K. OLUKOYA

- Power Against Destiny Quenchers
- Power Against Dream Criminals
0. Power Against Local Wickedness
1. Power Against Marine Spirits
)2. Power Against Spiritual Terrorists
)3. Power To Recover Your Lost Glory
04. Power To Disgrace The Oppressors
05. Power Must Change Hands (Prayer Points from 1995 - 2010)
06. Power To Shut Satanic Doors
07. Power Against The Mystery of Wickedness
108. Power of Brokenness
109. Pray Your Way To Breakthroughs
110. Prayer Passport
111. Prayer To Make You Fulfil Your Divine Destiny
112. Prayer Strategies For Spinsters And Bachelors
113. Prayer Warfare Against 70 Mad Spirits
114. Prayer Is The Battle
115. Prayer To Kill Enchantment and Divination
116. Prayer Rain

OTHER BOOKS BY DR. D. K. OLUKOYA

OTHER BOOKS BY DR. D. K. OLUKOYA

OTHER BOOKS BY DR. D. K. OLUKOYA

<u>OTHER BOOKS BY DR. D. K. OLUKOYA</u>

176. The Mystery Of Mobile Curses
177. The Mystery Of The Mobile Temple
178. The Prayer Eagle
179. The University of Champions
180. The Power of Aggressive Prayer Warriors
181. The Power of Priority
182. The Tongue Trap
183. The Terrible Agenda
184. The Scale of The Almighty
185. The Hidden Viper
186. The Star In Your Sky
187. The Star Hunters
188. The Spirit Of The Crab
189. The Snake In The Power House
190. The Slow Learners
191. The University of Champions
192. The Skeleton In Your Grandfather's Cupboard
193. The Serpentine Enemies
194. The Secrets Of Greatness
195. The Seasons Of Life

OTHER BOOKS BY DR. D. K. OLUKOYA

OTHER BOOKS BY DR. D. K. OLUKOYA

216. When God Is Silent
217. Where is Your Faith?
218. While Men Slept
219. Woman! Thou Art Loosed.
220. Why Problems Come Back
221. Your Battle And Your Strategy
222. Your Foundation And Destiny
223. Your Mouth and Your Deliverance
224. Your Mouth and Your Warfare

YORUBA PUBLICATION

1. Àdúrà Agbàyorí
2. Àdúrà Tí Nṣí Òkè Ní'dìí
3. Òjò Àdúrà

FRENCH PUBLICATIONS

1. Pluire De Prière
2. Espirit De Vagabondage
3. En Finir Avec Les Forces Maléfiques De La Maison De Ton Pére

23. Quand Les Choses Deviennent Difficiles
24. Les Stratégies De Prières Pour Les Cèlibataires
25. Se Libérer Des Alliances Maléfiques
26. Demanteler La Sorcellerie
27. La Déliverance: Le Flacon De Médicament De Dieu
28. La Dèliverance De La Tête
29. Commander Le Matin
30. Né Grand Mais Lié
31. Pouvoir Contre Les Démons Tropicaux
32. Le Proramme De Tranfert Des Richesse
33. Les Etudiants A l'ecole De La Peur
34. L'etoile Dans Votre Ciel
35. Les Saisons De La Vie
36. Femme Tu Es Liberee

ANNUAL 70 DAYS PRAYER & FASTING PUBLICATIONS

1. Prayers That Bring Miracles
2. Let God Answer By Fire
3. Prayers To Mount With Wings As Eagles
4. Prayers That Bring Explosive Increase

5. Prayers For Open Heavens
6. Prayers To Make You Fulfil Your Divine Destiny
7. Prayers That Make God To Answer And Fight By Fire
8. Prayers That Bring Unchallengeable Victory and Breakthrough Rainfall Bombardments
9. Prayers That Bring Dominion Prosperity And Uncommon Success
10. Prayers That Bring Power and Overflowing Progress
11. Prayers That Bring Laughter And Enlargement Breakthroughs
12. Prayers That Bring Uncommon Favour And Breakthroughs
13. Prayers That Bring Unprecedented Greatness & Unmatchable Increase
14. Prayers That Bring Awesome Testimonies And Turn Around Breakthroughs
15. Prayers To Secure Fresh Oil and Distinctive Shining.

When Your Foundation Needs Healing

THIS BOOK AND MORE ARE OBTAINABLE AT:

* MFM Bookshop Akeju
54, Akeju Street, Off Shipeolu Street, Onipanu, Lagos.
MFM Prayer City Branch
1st Floor, Modern Shopping Mall, MFM Prayer City
Km. 12, Lagos Ibadan Exp. Way, Ibafo, Ogun State.
* MFM International Bookshop
13, Olasimbo Street, Off Olumo Str., Onike, Yaba.

* The Battle Cry Christian Ministries
322, Herbert Macaulay Way, Sabo, Yaba, Lagos.

* IPFY Music Konnections Limited
48, Opebi Road, Salvation Bus Stop
Contact: 234-1-4719471, 234-8033056093

* All MFM Church branches nationwide and Christian bookstores.